STARGAZERS' GUIDES

Is There Life On Other Planets?

The Planets of our Solar System

Rosalind Mist

H www.heinemann.co.uk/library
Visit our website to find out more information about Heinemann Library books.

To order:
☎ Phone 44 (0) 1865 888066
▤ Send a fax to 44 (0) 1865 314091
▱ Visit the Heinemann Bookshop at www.heinemann.co.uk/library to browse our catalogue and order online.

First published in Great Britain by Heinemann Library, Halley Court, Jordan Hill, Oxford OX2 8EJ, part of Harcourt Education. Heinemann is a registered trademark of Harcourt Education Ltd.

Editorial: Nancy Dickmann and Sarah Chappelow
Design: Richard Parker and Tinstar Design
Illustrations: Jeff Edwards
Picture Research: Erica Newbery and Kay Altwegg
Production: Camilla Crask

Originated by Chroma Graphics (Overseas) Pte Ltd.
Printed in China by WKT Company Limited

10 digit ISBN: 0 431 18187 X
13 digit ISBN: 978 0 431 18187 5

10 09 08 07 06
10 9 8 7 6 5 4 3 2 1

British Library Cataloguing in Publication Data
Rosalind Mist
Is there life on other planets?
– (Stargazer guides)
523.4
A full catalogue record for this book is available from the British Library.

Acknowledgements
The publishers would like to thank the following for permission to reproduce photographs: Corbis pp. **9**, **34**, **37**; Galaxy pp. **10** (NASA/Robin Scagell),**16** (Robin Scagell), **17** (Jpl), **21** (NASA), **22** (Jpl), **24** (Jpl), **25** (Calvin J Hamilton), **27** (NASA/Robin Scagell), **28** (Jpl), **30** (Dave Tyler), **31** (Esa/NASA/University Of Arizona), **42** (Malin Space Science Systems); Getty Images/Photodisc pp. **8**, **19**, **32**; Science Photo Library pp. **4** (Detlev Van Ravenswaay), **7**, **11** (Gary Hincks), **12** (US Geological Survey), **13** (NASA JPL), **20** (Detlev Van Ravenswaay), **26**, **29** (John Chumack), **35**, **36**, **38**, **39** (Christian Darkin), **41** (Victor Habbick Visions), **43** (US Geological Survey); Science Photo Library/NASA pp. **14**, **15**, **33**, **40**; Touchstone Pictures p. **23** (Ronald Grant Archives).

Cover image of an alien landscape reproduced with permission of Corbis.

The publishers would like to thank Dr. Geza Gyuk of the Adler Planetarium in Chicago for his assistance in the preparation of this book.

Every effort has been made to contact copyright holders of any material reproduced in this book. Any omissions will be rectified in subsequent printings if notice is given to the publishers.

The paper used to print this book comes from sustainable resources.

Contents

Words appearing in the text in bold, **like this**, are explained in the Glossary.

The Solar System

The Earth is just one of the planets in our **Solar System**. The Sun, our nearest star, is the centre of the Solar System and has nine planets orbiting it. In turn, the planets have over 157 **moons** orbiting them. As there are still new moons being discovered, this could rise to over 160. The Solar System is huge. The distance from the Sun to Pluto (the outermost planet) is on average 5.9 billion kilometres (3.6 billion miles).

Rocky and gas planets

The planets in the Solar System are all different from each other, but there are clearly two different types. These are the terrestrial or rocky planets and the giant gas planets. The terrestrial planets are smaller, rocky planets, like Earth. There are four of them: Mercury, Venus, Earth, and Mars. The gas planets are much, much bigger. They do not have solid surfaces, as they are made of gas. The four gas planets are Jupiter, Saturn, Uranus, and Neptune.

In our Solar System, nine planets and millions of asteroids orbit the Sun.

Sun   Mercury   Venus Earth Mars   Jupiter

Pluto is the ninth planet, and is not a rocky planet or a gas planet. It is small and has a solid surface and is even further away from the Sun than the gas planets. Between the rocky and the gas planets is the **asteroid** belt. Here many lumps of small rock orbit around the Sun. They are sometimes called minor planets.

The search for life

The only place in the Solar System where we know there is life is the Earth. However, scientists are looking in all sorts of unusual places for the chemicals needed for life. They are searching asteroids, **comets**, moons, and the other planets. Our Solar System isn't the only one in the **Universe**. Astronomers have discovered many more planets around other stars. Maybe there is life on one of these!

Despite their similarities, all the planets look different. Earth has land and water, and Mars is a rocky reddish desert. Neptune is a lovely blue and Saturn is a pinkish colour.

TRY IT YOURSELF:
Remember the planets

Can you make a mnemonic to help you remember the order of the planets? The first letter of each word in a mnemonic is the same as the first letter of the words in the phrase you want to remember. Starting from the Sun, the order of the planets is Mercury, Venus, Earth, Mars, Jupiter, Saturn, Uranus, Neptune, and Pluto. Here is a mnemonic to get you started: My Very Energetic Mongoose Just Swam Under the North Pole.

Saturn   **Uranus   Neptune   Pluto**

Keeping it all together

Have you ever wondered why the planets orbit around the Sun, or why the Moon orbits the Earth? It's all to do with **gravity**. But what does that really mean? To find out, let's look at the work of Isaac Newton (1642–1727), the scientist who worked out the laws of gravity.

Imagine being Isaac Newton, sitting under an apple tree. He asked a good question: why do apples fall to the ground and not hover in space? Newton decided that there must be something pulling the apples towards the Earth, and he called it the force of gravity. He realized that gravity keeps us attached to the Earth, so that we don't fall off and drift into space.

Gravity is one of the forces of nature. More massive objects have a stronger gravitational pull.

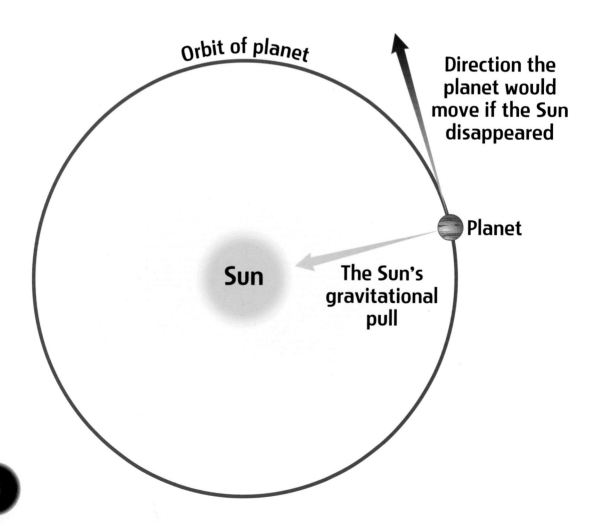

Orbit of planet

Direction the planet would move if the Sun disappeared

Planet

Sun

The Sun's gravitational pull

Newton realized that Earth's gravity extends out to the Moon. The bigger planets have lots of moons orbiting around them, kept there by gravity.

Being massive

Newton worked out that any two objects are attracted to each other by gravity. The strength of gravity between them depends on the **masses** of the objects involved and how far apart they are. As the Earth is so massive, it has a strong gravitational pull.

But what about the Sun? The Sun is really, really massive. You could fit over a million Earths inside it. Newton realized that it must have a much stronger gravitational pull than Earth. Its gravity tugs at the Earth and all the other planets in the Solar System.

HOW IT WORKS:
Why don't the planets crash?

If the Sun is so massive, why doesn't it pull the planets into it? Newton had already worked out that if something is moving, it won't stop or change direction unless there is a force that makes it do so. Imagine the Earth trying to move past the Sun in a straight line. As the Earth moves along, the Sun pulls it a bit towards it. The Earth carries on trying to move in a straight line, but the Sun keeps pulling. The Earth doesn't get closer to the Sun, it just starts to bend round in a curve. As the Sun pulls and the Earth keeps moving, the curve carries on and on, taking the Earth in a big circle around the Sun. In the same way, the other planets are kept in orbit round the Sun, and the Moon stays in orbit around the Earth.

Life on Earth

Earth is a very special planet – it is the only place in the Solar System where we know life exists. No one has found any evidence of life forms elsewhere in the Solar System, or in the Universe. If we do ever discover life elsewhere in the Solar System, it probably won't be little green men. It is much more likely that there will be **microbes**. These could be still alive, or they may be extinct.

The life forms that have **evolved** on Earth need **carbon**, **organic chemicals**, and water, as well as a source of **energy**. Life elsewhere in the Universe might need all these things, or it might need very different conditions.

Water

About 70 per cent of the Earth is covered in water. Without this water, we would not be alive today. Scientists believe that water is a key ingredient for life, as it can dissolve many chemicals. Finding water on a planet or moon does not mean that there is life there, but it does make life possible.

The Earth is unique in the Solar System. It is the only place where we know life exists.

Some **bacteria** can live in very hot places, like these thermal springs that can reach over 80 °C (177 °F).

Other chemicals

We also need certain chemicals to help us live. Carbon is a special **atom** that can attach itself to many other atoms to form **molecules**. Some of these molecules can dissolve in water, something else that is important for life. Carbon helps to build the more complicated molecules, called organic chemicals, that scientists find in all life forms.

Energy

Organisms need a source of energy to live. For most of the life on Earth, this comes from the Sun. The Sun heats the Earth to the right temperature to keep water liquid in lots of places. Light from the Sun is also used in a chemical reaction called **photosynthesis** to create enough energy for plants to grow. Animals get energy from food that they eat. This can be from plants or animals.

HOT NEWS:
Strange lives

Life on Earth doesn't just exist in forests and oceans. There are some very strange places where life has been found. For example, microbes have been found in rocks thousands of metres below the Earth's surface. They have also been discovered in extremely dry desert conditions and around thermal vents deep in the oceans.

The rocky planets

Earth is one of the four rocky or inner planets: Mercury, Venus, Earth, and Mars. Closest to the Sun is Mercury, followed by Venus, Earth, and Mars. The orbits of the rocky planets are grouped much more closely together than those of the gas planets. It is 78 million km (49 million miles) between the orbits of Earth and Mars, but about 650 million km (405 million miles) between the orbits of Jupiter and Saturn.

Small and dense

Compared with the gas planets, the four rocky planets are all small. Neptune, the smallest of the gas planets, is nearly four times the **diameter** of Earth, the largest of the rocky planets. The rocky planets are also **denser** than the gas planets. This means that lump of a rocky planet weighs more than a lump of a gas planet of the same size.

Mercury, Venus, and Mars all have cratered surfaces, but Venus's atmosphere hides its surface.

Mercury   Venus   Earth   Mars

Similarities and differences

Each of the rocky planets has a very similar structure. At the centre of each planet is an iron **core**, surrounded by a thicker layer called the **mantle**. Outside the mantle is a thin, rocky **crust**.

Venus and Earth are about the same size and both have quite thick **atmospheres**. They even have similar densities and are made up of similar **elements**. Venus and Earth are sometimes called the sister planets.

Although there are lots of similarities between the four rocky planets, there are plenty of differences too. Mercury has hardly any atmosphere, while the atmosphere on Venus is particularly thick. And no planet other than Earth still has liquid water on the surface.

TRY IT YOURSELF:
A Solar System model

On a dry, calm day, find a new, clean toilet roll or other roll of paper with sheets and 10 marbles. You'll also need a large space, maybe a playing field or a large hall. Start at one end of the field. Place a marble on the end of the roll of paper to secure it: this is the Sun. Now unroll your paper, counting the sheets of paper as you go. The chart below tells you how far each of the planets is from the Sun. Put a marble on the paper every time you get to a planet. This activity shows you how far apart the planets are, but not the relative sizes of the planets.

Core **Crust** **Mantle**

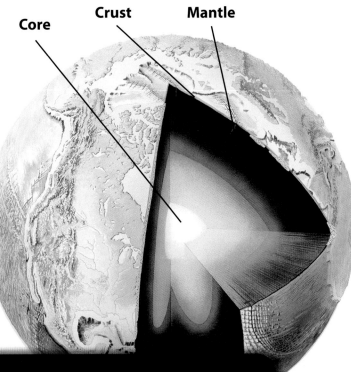

The rocky planets are all small and dense with similar structures.

Planet	Sheets of paper
Mercury	1
Venus	2
Earth	2.5
Mars	4
Jupiter	13
Saturn	24
Uranus	49
Neptune	77
Pluto	100

Mercury

The smallest rocky planet is Mercury. It is not much bigger than the Moon and the surface is covered in **craters**. It takes Mercury 88 days to orbit the Sun, and 59 days to **rotate** once. Because Mercury rotates so slowly on its **axis**, but orbits so quickly, by the time it has done a complete rotation, the Sun is in a different place. This means that a day, from sunrise to sunset, lasts about two Mercury years, or 176 days!

Hot and cold

Mercury is the closest planet to the Sun. It is so close that it can get very hot. At its hottest, the surface of the planet facing the Sun reaches 427 °C (801 °F). This is hot enough to melt tin and lead. At night, the surface of Mercury cools down. On Earth, the temperature might drop by 10–20 degrees at night. However, on Mercury it is dark for much longer, and Mercury has a much thinner atmosphere. This means that the surface gets *much* cooler. The temperature can drop to –170 °C (–270 °F). This makes Mercury both one of the hottest and one of the coldest bodies in the Solar System!

Mercury is covered in craters, just like the Moon.

On the surface

Mercury has an interesting surface. There are highland and lowland areas. The highlands are bumpy and covered in craters. In between these craters are the lowland areas, which are smoother and look like gently rolling countryside. Scientists think that the lowland plains could have formed from lava (molten rock). The lava would have broken through the surface after the craters were formed and covered up the lowland areas.

HOT NEWS:

Caloris Basin is one of the largest craters on Mercury. It's about 1340 km (833 miles) across. This is about the size of France and Germany put together! The gigantic asteroid that caused the crater was about 150 km (93 miles) across. The impact was so great that an area on the opposite side of the planet was damaged in a large Mercury-quake. This would be like a crash happening at the North Pole and causing an earthquake at the South Pole.

Mercury fact file	
Rotation period	59 days
Length of year	88 days
Distance from the Sun	58 million km (36 million miles)
Diameter	4880 km (3032 miles)
Number of moons	0

Rim of the Caloris Basin

When this photo of Mercury was taken, only half of the Caloris Basin was visible. The other half was in shadow.

Mercury mysteries

There are several scientific mysteries about Mercury. One of the biggest mysteries is why it is so much denser than the other rocky planets. The heaviest part of the rocky planets is the core. It is heavy because it has a lot of metal in it. The cores of the planets are different sizes. The core of the Earth takes up about 35 per cent of the planet. As Mercury is so dense, this could mean that the core is about 65 per cent of the total volume of the planet. It has been suggested that Mercury used to have a larger rocky mantle surrounding the core, but that the Sun has **vaporized** most of it (turned it to gas). Another suggestion is that a giant asteroid hit Mercury a long time ago and sent most of its rocky layer out into space.

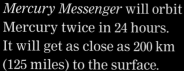

Mercury Messenger will orbit Mercury twice in 24 hours. It will get as close as 200 km (125 miles) to the surface.

Mercury's magnetic field

Another mystery about Mercury is its **magnetic field**. The spacecraft *Mariner 10* showed that Mercury's magnetic field seems to be a miniature version of the Earth's. This was unexpected. The Earth's magnetic field is caused by iron in the core swirling around, but scientists had thought that Mercury's core was solid. Mercury's magnetic field suggests that the core might still be liquid. Another possibility is that the core is a bit like a magnetized needle. When the swirling stopped, the core became a giant magnetic needle. A magnetic needle gets less magnetic over time, so perhaps Mercury is gradually becoming less magnetic.

HOT NEWS:
Mercury Messengers

Mercury Messenger is the next mission to Mercury. It will arrive in 2011 after a journey of 6.5 years. It will be the first spacecraft to visit Mercury since 1975. Scientists hope that the NASA spacecraft will help them to work out why Mercury is so dense. *Bepi Columbo* is another mission to Mercury and is due to be launched in 2012. It will have two parts: one that will map the surface of the planet and one that will study its magnetic field. *Bepi Colombo* is a joint project between Europe and Japan.

Mercury Messenger was launched from Cape Canaveral Air Force Station, Florida, USA on 3 August 2004.

Venus

Venus is the second planet from the Sun. It takes 225 days to go around the Sun, but it takes 243 days to rotate on its axis. So a day on Venus lasts longer than a year! Venus is the nearest planet to Earth. Like Earth, it has an atmosphere, but the atmosphere of Venus is very different to ours. The most common gas in Earth's atmosphere is **nitrogen**, but about 98 per cent of Venus' atmosphere is **carbon dioxide**. The clouds on Venus are made of sulphuric acid, not water. It would be no fun to get caught out in the rain on Venus!

Looking through the clouds

One similarity between Venus' atmosphere and Earth's is that there are lots of clouds. However, the clouds on Venus are very thick and cover the whole of the planet. This creates a few problems for space explorers, as the clouds block the view of the surface. However, scientists have come up with other ways to find out what the surface looks like. They have either sent spacecraft to land on the planet, or they have used radar.

Venus is best seen around sunrise and sunset. It is sometimes called the Morning or Evening Star.

Using radar

Radar stands for radio detection and ranging. It is a way of looking through clouds using radio waves. A spacecraft flying over Venus sends a beam of radio waves down to the surface. The waves bounce off Venus and back to the spacecraft. The spacecraft can get information from the returning radio wave about the surface of Venus. Between 1992 and 1994, a space probe called *Magellan* orbited Venus. The radar images it took showed that the surface was covered in craters and volcanoes.

TRY IT YOURSELF: **Find Venus**

After the Sun and the Moon, Venus is the brightest object you can see in the sky. Just after sunset or before sunrise, look for the brightest "star" in the sky, and what you are looking at will be Venus. It used to be thought that Venus was actually two stars, called the Morning Star and the Evening Star. We now know that it is a planet that is best seen at around sunrise and sunset. Venus can also be seen during the day, but never point binoculars or a telescope in the direction of the Sun. Visit www.heavens-above.com to find out when you can see Venus.

Venus fact file	
Rotation period	243 days
Length of year	225 days
Distance from the Sun	108 million km (67 millions miles)
Diameter	12,104 km (7521 miles)
Number of moons	0

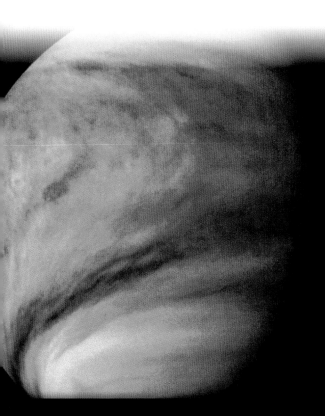

Clouds, made of sulphuric acid, swirl around in Venus' dense atmosphere.

Global warming

You might think that the hottest planet in the Solar System would be Mercury, as it is closest to the Sun. But Venus is hotter than Mercury. This is because Venus has a thick atmosphere, while Mercury has virtually none. Venus' atmosphere acts like a big blanket, which keeps the heat of the Sun in. The carbon dioxide atmosphere is about 100 times more dense than Earth's. Carbon dioxide is one of the greenhouse gases that traps heat. Because of this atmosphere, the temperature on Venus can reach 464 °C (867 °F).

Our atmosphere

Venus isn't the only planet whose atmosphere keeps it warm. Earth's atmosphere contains nitrogen, **oxygen**, and a tiny bit of carbon dioxide (0.035%). Our atmosphere is thick enough and contains enough greenhouse gases to raise the surface temperature on Earth by about 30 °C (86 °F). Without it, the planet would be frozen.

HOW IT WORKS:

In a greenhouse, the glass lets sunlight in, but does not let heat out. The Sun heats up the soil and the air inside, but the heat is trapped by the glass and cannot escape. This is very similar to how the greenhouse effect works on the planets. Sunlight heats the surface of a planet. In a planet without an atmosphere, this heat **radiates** back into space. On Venus and Earth, the heat from the surface also radiates outward, but it has to pass through the atmosphere before it reaches space. The carbon dioxide and other greenhouse gases in the atmosphere absorb the heat. These gases then radiate the heat back to the surface.

Sun

Some solar energy reflected by the planet back out to space

Planet's surface heats up and sends heat back into space. Greenhouse gases trap some of the heat around the planet.

Energy from Sun passes through atmosphere

Atmosphere

Venus

Most radiation is absorbed by the planet's surface and warms it

Infrared radiation is emitted from the planet's surface

Venus gets very warm because the atmosphere keeps in heat from the Sun.

Earth is getting hotter

The Earth's temperature is gradually rising. Although the Earth's temperature has risen and fallen over the years, scientists believe that it is rising unusually fast. They think that it is because the atmosphere has more and more greenhouse gases in it, mainly extra carbon dioxide. The carbon dioxide comes from burning fossil fuels such as coal, oil, and gas.

Life on Venus?

Imagine trying to live on Venus. It has little oxygen and it rains sulphuric acid. It can get hot enough to melt lead, but the clouds block out direct Sun. It really isn't a place that could support life as we know it.

A Soviet spacecraft, the *Venera 13 Lander*, landed on Venus in 1982. It took 14 pictures of the surface, which were used to create this image.

Mars

Mars is the fourth planet from the Sun, and is about half the diameter of Earth. A day on Mars is a similar length to a day on Earth, but its year is much longer. Mars takes about twice as long as Earth to orbit the Sun. Also, its orbit is more **elliptical** (oval) than that of the other planets. This means that the temperature changes between summer and winter are much greater than on Earth.

Mars is 228 million km (142 million miles) from the Sun, so it is colder than Earth. The temperature can drop to –140 °C (–220 °F) at night and it is rarely above freezing during the day. As on Venus the atmosphere is mostly carbon dioxide, but it is much thinner and there are no clouds of sulphuric acid.

The Valles Marineris is so large that it would stretch all the way across the USA. In places, it reaches 600 km (375 miles) wide.

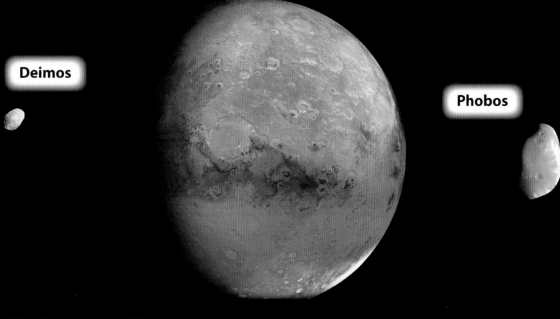

Deimos

Phobos

Phobos and Deimos are small moons. They are not big enough for gravity to have pulled them into a spherical shape.

The surface of Mars

When we look at Mars in the sky, it appears to be red. This is because the soil on the surface of Mars contains a lot of iron oxide (rust).

Mars has two of the most spectacular features in the Solar System. The giant valley Valles Marineris is over 3000 km (1850 miles) long and up to 8 km (5 miles) deep. This is nearly four times longer and over four times deeper that the Grand Canyon in the USA. Olympus Mons is the Solar System's largest volcano. The top of the volcano is 25 km (15 miles) high. This is nearly three times higher than Mount Everest!

Martian moons

Mars has two tiny moons called Phobos and Deimos. Phobos is only 21 km (13 miles) in diameter, while Deimos is only 12 km (7 miles). The moons were probably once asteroids that came too close to Mars and got trapped by its gravity.

TRY IT YOURSELF:
Check out the red planet

Mars can be seen with the naked eye and is red when you look at it. You cannot see much detail, even if you look at Mars with binoculars or a small telescope. The most you can expect to see are the light ice patches near the **poles**. The best views of Mars are seen when it comes close to Earth, which happens every two years.

Water on Mars

Water is an essential substance for life, and there is plenty of it on Mars. At least, there is plenty of ice. There are ice caps covering most of the north and the south poles. But Mars' ice is not frozen water, like the ice caps in the Arctic and Antarctic. Mars' ice is mostly frozen carbon dioxide, with a bit of frozen water mixed in.

As on Earth, Mars' size of the ice caps changes depending on the season. In the winter, they grow as it gets colder. When the weather gets warmer in the summer, the ice caps get smaller. However, the differences between summer and winter are much greater on Mars, so the ice caps shrink and grow much more.

Mars fact file	
Rotation period	24.6 hours
Length of year	687 days
Distance from the Sun	228 million km (142 million miles)
Diameter	6794 km (4222 miles)
Number of moons	2

The polar ice caps shrink in the summer, revealing the surface underneath.

Water below the surface

The ice caps are not the only place where water is found on Mars. Scientists have found frozen water below the surface. Scientists think that there may even be liquid water underground.

Liquid water

There are stripy Martian rocks that seem to have been made in layers, just like some rocks on Earth. These rocks could be layers of lava, or mud, or sand from seas or rivers. Some of the stripy rocks have layers that are only 1cm (0.5 inch) across. Scientists think that the stripes are too thin to be lava. They think that they look like sedimentary rocks on Earth. Sedimentary rocks form at the bottom of rivers or oceans when mud and sand settle underwater. So there may once have been liquid water on the surface of Mars.

SCIENCE FACT OR SCIENCE FICTION?

In 1877, the Italian astronomer Giovani Schiaparelli saw some straight line markings on the surface of Mars. He described them as *canali* ("channels"). People made a mistake when they translated this and thought that he meant canals – artificial rivers. The US astronomer Percival Lowell made many observations of Mars, and mapped 500 "canals". In 1895 he published a book suggesting that the canals were built by Martians to support farming life on the planet. In 1964, the *Mariner 4* spacecraft showed that these "canals" do not exist. However, scientists have now found channels on Mars that could be dried-up rivers.

Hollywood film directors often turn the surface of Mars very red. The actual surface is more of a brown-red colour.

The gas planets

Imagine travelling in a spacecraft starting from the Sun. First, you pass the orbits of the rocky planets, Mercury, Venus, Earth, and Mars. Then you cross the asteroid belt, filled with millions of rocks orbiting the Sun. Next, 779 million km (484 million miles) from the Sun, you come across another planet. It's very different from any you have seen before, it's a gas giant.

Four gas planets

The four gas planets (Jupiter, Saturn, Uranus, and Neptune) are balls of rotating gas and dust. They are mainly made of gases like **hydrogen** and **helium**. Both the rocky planets and the gas giants probably formed with gas clouds surrounding them. The planets near the Sun got hot enough for most of the gas cloud to escape from the planets' gravitational pull and disappear into space. The gas planets got much less heat, so the gases around them stayed in place.

Between 1981 and 1989, the *Voyager 2* space probe visited all the giant gas planets. It is the only spacecraft to have done this.

The giant planets

Although the gas giants are huge, they are still quite a bit smaller than the Sun. The biggest planet in the Solar System is Jupiter, but 1000 Jupiters would fit inside the Sun. The gas planets are less dense than the rocky planets. This is because they are mostly made of gas, which is very light. Saturn would even float in water, if we could find an ocean large enough! However, they are so much larger than the rocky planets that they are more massive (they contain more matter).

Rings and moons

One feature common to all the giant planets is that they all have rings around them. These rings are made of ice, dust, and small rocks. They also all have many moons.

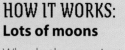

HOW IT WORKS:
Lots of moons

Why do the gas giants have so many moons? They are massive planets, so their gravitational pull is very strong. Their gravity affects a large area of space – more than the gravity of the rocky planets. Many asteroids have been trapped by the gravity of one of the gas planets. They become moons, orbiting the planet.

Surprisingly, the gravitational pull at the surface of a giant planet is similar to that on Earth. This is because the gravitational pull depends on how far you are from the centre of the planet. Because the gas planets are so big, the surface is further from the centre, so the pull at the surface is lower than you might expect.

The gas giants don't have a solid surface. If you tried to stand on the planet, you would fall through the atmosphere until you get to the rocky core.

Jupiter

Jupiter is the largest planet in the Solar System. You could fit 11 Earths across the middle of Jupiter and still have space left over. Even though Jupiter is so big, it rotates amazingly fast. A day on Jupiter is only 10 hours long. Jupiter rotates so fast that it bulges out at the **equator**.

In the core

Like all the giant planets, Jupiter is a gassy planet with a rocky iron core. The core is very hot – the temperature there could be 30,000 °C (50,000 °F). Around the core is a very dense layer of hydrogen, then a layer of liquid hydrogen and helium.

The stripy patterns we see on Jupiter are the clouds in its atmosphere.

Jupiter fact file	
Rotation period	9.8 hours
Length of year	12 years
Distance from the Sun	778 million km (484 million miles)
Diameter	142,984 km (88,846 miles)
Number of moons	at least 63

TRY IT YOURSELF:
Jupiter and its moons

Once Venus has set, Jupiter is usually the brightest object in the sky. It is visible nearly all night and most of the year. Use a small telescope or binoculars to look at Jupiter. You should be able to see that it is slightly elliptical, because it bulges at the equator as it spins. You should also be able to see some of the four biggest moons, which were discovered by the Italian scientist Galileo (1564–1642). Watch for the moons over several nights. Record how many you see each night, and where they are. They will appear in different places as they orbit Jupiter.

The Great Red Spot is about twice as big as Earth.

Storms in the atmosphere

When we look at Jupiter we see the gassy atmosphere, which is full of clouds. These are dark if they are lower down and light if they are higher up. The temperature at the top of the clouds is a cool −130 °C. There are many storms in Jupiter's atmosphere. The most obvious one is an area called the Great Red Spot. This is an enormous storm, like a hurricane on Earth. However, this hurricane is more than twice as big as the Earth itself. The storm has been raging for at least 300 years and was first seen in 1664.

Rings at Jupiter

Just like Saturn and the other giant planets, Jupiter has rings of rocky, icy material around it. Jupiter's rings are not as impressive as the rings of Saturn, but they are still an incredible sight. Jupiter also has a very strong magnetic field. This is so big that it reaches out beyond the orbit of Saturn.

Jupiter's moons

The rocky planets do not have many moons. The Earth has one, Mars has two, and Venus and Mercury do not have any. The gas planets make up for this. Amazingly, Jupiter has over 60 moons, with more still being discovered. The four biggest are called the Galilean moons after the great Italian scientist Galileo (see box on page 29).

The Galilean moons

The four Galilean moons are called Io, Europa, Ganymede, and Callisto. Io is so close to Jupiter that Jupiter's gravity creates tides. The tides are not in seas – they are movements of the ground! The pull of Jupiter's gravity moves the whole moon's surface up and down by about 100 metres (330 feet). This rising and falling creates a lot of heat energy and melts the inside of Io, so the surface is covered with volcanoes.

Europa is the next closest Galilean moon. This is an icy moon. Scientists think that Jupiter's gravity may also move Europa's surface up and down. This might create enough heat to melt some ice trapped below the surface. There may be liquid underground oceans, and these could contain life.

Europa is the smoothest Galilean moon. It is covered in an icy crust.

Ganymede is the third and largest Galilean moon. It is the largest moon in the Solar System, bigger than Mercury and Pluto. Even though it is so large, it is called a moon because it orbits a planet, not the Sun. Ganymede is another icy moon that may have an ocean of water below the surface.

The final Galilean moon is Callisto. Callisto has a giant crater called Valhalla, which is 3000 km (1865 miles) across.

Other moons

Jupiter has many other moons. The smallest is only 1.6 km (1 mile) across. Two of Jupiter's moons, Meta and Adrastea, are even closer to Jupiter than Io. One day, Jupiter's gravity will pull Meta and Adastrea into the planet.

Galilean moons	
Moon	Diameter
Io	3630 km (2555 miles)
Europa	3140 km (1850 miles)
Ganymede	5250 km (3260 miles)
Callisto	4800 km (2985 miles)

Saturn

Saturn is the sixth planet from the Sun. Like all the giant planets, it has an iron core, with gases around the edge. Saturn takes just 10 hours to rotate, so a day is even shorter than on Jupiter. However, it takes 29.5 years to orbit the Sun, so the year is longer. Saturn is 95 times more massive (heavy) than Earth. This means that the pull of its gravity is much stronger. But gravity at Saturn's surface is lower than on the Earth, because Saturn is nearly ten times larger than the Earth.

Saturn's gassy atmosphere is made of hydrogen and helium, as on Jupiter. Winds in the atmosphere can reach 1600 km/h (1000 mph). Saturn doesn't have a big red spot, but there are plenty of storms. The biggest of these are twice as big as on the Earth, and appear about every 30 years.

Like all the giant planets, Saturn has lots of moons. They are icy and rocky.

Titan is the second largest moon in the Solar System, after Ganymede.

Moons, moons, moons

Saturn has 34 known moons, and more are being discovered all the time. Titan is the largest. At 5150 km (3200 miles) across, Titan is slightly bigger than Mercury. It has an atmosphere, mostly made of nitrogen but with some other gases mixed in. It is probably very similar to Earth's atmosphere billions of years ago. Titan's atmosphere is so dense that we cannot see the surface from above.

One of Saturn's other moons is Phoebe. This moon is similar to the planet Pluto. It has a similar density, and is probably a mixture of ice and rock. Two of Saturn's moons, Epimetheus and Janus, are almost in the same orbit. One is slightly closer to Saturn than the other, but not always the same one. Every few years they swap positions, without bumping into each other!

Saturn fact file	
Rotation period	10.2 hours
Length of year	29.5 years
Distance from the Sun	1.43 billion km (887 million miles)
Diameter	120,536 km (74,898 miles)
Number of moons	at least 34

Saturn's rings

Saturn's rings are its most spectacular feature and have been admired for hundreds of years. The first person to see the rings was Galileo in 1610, but he didn't know what they were. He thought they were two other objects near to Saturn. In 1655, Christiaan Huygens observed Saturn with a larger telescope and proposed that they were rings. Using bigger and bigger telescopes on Earth, astronomers eventually found three rings. Today, space probes and the Hubble Space Telescope have shown us how complicated the rings really are.

Saturn's rings have lots of details hidden in them. Some of the rings have wavy edges.

BIOGRAPHY:

Giovani Domenico Cassini (1625 – 1712)

Giovanni Cassini was born in Italy. He was the first of a whole family of astronomers. Cassini made many important discoveries during his life. He discovered Jupiter's Red Spot and worked out how long a day lasts on Jupiter. He was also the first person to observe four of Saturn's moons. He even discovered the gap between Saturn's A and B rings. This is called the *Cassini division* in his honour.

Dust, rock and ice

Saturn's rings are are over 282,000 km (175,000 miles) wide, but they are no more than 100 metres thick. They are made up of dust, rock, and ice. The largest bits are boulders, a few metres wide. Some parts of the rings are denser than others, with dust and gas gathering together in clumps.

All the material in the ring system weighs no more than Mimas, one of Saturn's smaller moons. Scientists think that the rings could be the remains of one or more moons of Saturn that were bashed into smaller and smaller pieces. They also think that they finished forming before Saturn itself.

Gaps between the rings

The three brightest sections of Saturn's rings, which are visible from Earth, are called the A ring (the outermost one), the B ring, and the C ring. Between the A and B rings is what seems from Earth to be a gap, called the Cassini division. In fact we now know that there are faint rings within the Cassini division.

Shepherd moons

Outside the A ring is a thin, bright ring called the F ring, which cannot be seen from Earth. This ring is thin because it is hemmed in by two small moons, called Prometheus and Pandora. These two moons are called 'shepherd moons' because they keep the pieces of rock in a narrow ring.

Cassini is taking pictures of Saturn, its rings, and its moons.

Uranus

Uranus was discovered in 1781 by William Herschel. It was the first planet to be discovered using a telescope. Unlike the previous six planets, it cannot be seen with the naked eye. Like Jupiter and Saturn, Uranus rotates quite fast, despite being 51,118 km (31,763 miles) across. A day on Uranus is just 17 hours long. This means it looks like a squashed circle, or an ellipse.

A tilting planet

Uranus has one very surprising feature, it is tilted by 98 degrees. This means that its poles can point towards the Sun. If you were going to make a human model of the Solar System, you might have someone standing in the middle being the Sun. You'd then place people around the Sun and set them spinning on the spot, before asking them to start walking round, or orbiting, the Sun. However, to be Uranus, you would have to lie on the floor and roll around on the spot and be dragged around the Sun at the same time! No-one is quite sure why Uranus is so different. It may have been hit by another big planet billions of years ago, soon after the formation of the Solar System.

Uranus looks slightly green, due to the methane in its atmosphere. Like the other gas giants, Uranus has a ring system.

Rings and moons

The rings of Uranus were discovered in 1977. The first images of the rings were taken in 1986 by the *Voyager 2* space probe. Hubble Space Telescope has since taken images of the rings. The rings are darker than Saturn's rings. They are made of dust and small particles.

Uranus has 27 moons. The first five were discovered between 1787 and 1948. All the moons are quite small. Miranda is the strangest moon. It has a very dramatic surface, with cliffs and craters. It might even have ice welling up from the surface.

BIOGRAPHY:
William Herschel (1738–1822)

William Herschel worked as a musician and composer until the age of 40, when he began to study the skies. He designed and built his own telescopes, which were the most powerful in the world at that time. As well as discovering Uranus in 1781, Herschel also discovered several of Saturn's moons and worked out the motion of binary stars. These are stars that orbit each other.

William Herschel was looking for stars when he discovered Uranus. His sister, Caroline, was also an excellent astronomer. She was the first woman to be elected a member of the Royal Society.

Uranus fact file	
Rotation period	17 hours
Length of year	84 years
Distance from the Sun	2.9 billion km (1.8 billion miles)
Diameter	51,118 km (31,763 miles)
Number of moons	at least 27

Neptune

After the discovery of Uranus, scientists spent a long time observing the planet and working out its orbit. From Newton's laws of gravity, they knew how Uranus should orbit. But Uranus' orbit did not fit with the predictions. Scientists guessed that there must be another planet out there, pulling at Uranus and changing the shape of its orbit. The mystery planet was discovered on 23 September 1846 by Johann Galle and Heinrich d'Arrest. It became known as Neptune. Neptune is so far away that it takes 164 years to orbit the Sun, but again it has a very short day – just over 16 hours.

The Great Dark Spot was seen in 1989 by the *Voyager 2* spacecraft, but it had disappeared by 1994, when the Hubble Space Telescope looked at Neptune. It had been replaced by another dark spot.

Neptune fact file	
Rotation period	16.1 hours
Length of year	164 years
Distance from the Sun	4498 million km (2800 million miles)
Diameter	49,528 km (30,775 miles)
Number of moons	at least 13

HOW IT WORKS:

The giant planets all have clouds, as do Venus and the Earth. Clouds on the Earth are made from **water vapour** that has risen through the atmosphere until it is cool enough to become tiny droplets of water. If it is cold enough, the water droplets turn into ice crystals. Clouds on other planets form in the same way. Gases rise through the atmosphere and eventually cool and turn into droplets or ice. However, clouds on the other planets are not just made from water. It is so cold on Jupiter and Saturn that some of the clouds are made from substances that are gases on Earth, such as ammonia. Uranus and Neptune are cold enough to have methane (natural gas) ice clouds.

Triton

The first moon of Neptune was discovered shortly after the planet itself, on 10 October 1846. It is an unusual moon because it orbits Neptune backwards. This means that the moon is travelling in the opposite direction to the way the planet spins. The new moon was not named for 60 years, but it was eventually called Triton. Astronomers have now found twelve other moons around Neptune.

Triton is smaller than the Moon (2710 km or 1685 miles across) but it is larger than Pluto. The surface of Triton seems to be volcanic. In most places in the Solar System, being volcanic means that there is molten rock coming out of the surface. However, on Triton, it looks like there is a mixture of ice and slush erupting from the surface.

The surface of Triton does not have many craters. These may have been covered by the volcanic ice.

Pluto

Pluto was discovered in 1930 by a young US astronomer called Clyde W. Tombaugh. As Pluto is so small and so far away, it is taking a long time for astronomers to find out many details about this planet. Up until now, astronomers have only been able to study Pluto using telescopes. No spacecraft have visited this planet.

Pluto has a diameter of about 2274 km (1413 miles). This is about two-thirds the diameter of the Moon. In 1978, astronomers discovered that Pluto has a moon, called Charon. Charon is about a third the size of Pluto (1190 km, 740 miles in diameter).

Pluto is named after the God of the underworld of the dead and Charon is named after the old boatman who ferried souls to Pluto's underworld realm.

Charon

Pluto

Pluto fact file	
Rotation period	6.39 days
Length of year	248 years
Distance from the Sun	5.9 billion km (3.7 billion miles)
Diameter	2274 km (1413 miles)
Number of moons	1

The tenth planet?

There have been several recent discoveries of large, planet-like objects orbiting around the Sun. These are all further away than Pluto.

One was discovered in November 2003. It is unofficially called Sedna and is about 1700 km (1055 miles) in diameter. Sedna is about twice as far away as Pluto. In 2005, scientists announced the discovery of two new objects, both of which were first observed in 2003. Probably smaller than Pluto is 2003 EL61. Not much else is known about this object, and scientists are working hard to find out more information about it. 2003 UB313 is about 3000 km (1865 miles) across, which makes it bigger than Pluto. The object is in the Kuiper Belt, about three times as far away from the Sun as Pluto.

Rock and ice

Pluto is made of rock and ice, so it is not really like either the rocky planets, which are made of rock and iron, or the gas planets, which are mostly hydrogen and helium, with iron cores.

Most planets move around the Sun in orbits that are very close to, but not quite, circles. Pluto's orbit is a little bit different. It is much more elliptical than the orbits of other planets and it is tilted at an angle to the orbits of the other planets. Pluto even moves closer to the Sun than Neptune for about 20 years of its 248-year orbit. It might seem possible that Neptune and Pluto could crash into each other when they swap over, but scientists have worked out that this is never going to happen.

Sedna is an unofficial name for an object officially named 2003 VB12. It is named after the Inuit

Life in the Solar System

Could there be life elsewhere in the Solar System? Well, we haven't found any yet, but it is possible that the conditions for life exist somewhere else in the Solar System. However, this life would have evolved under conditions very different to those on Earth. Alien life could look very different and might not necessarily need all the same ingredients as we do (water, organic chemicals, and energy). Scientists don't think that they will find Martians on Mars, but possibly there might be microbes, such as bacteria or fungi there. These alien life forms could use energy from chemicals in the water they live in, warm rocks at the middle of the planet or from the Sun.

Weird life

From what we have already learned about other planets, none of them seem to have very good conditions in which life could develop. However, we are discovering strange kinds of life on Earth, in places where in the past no-one thought life could exist. For example, rock-eating microbes have been found deep under the Earth's surface, away from the Sun, and there are microbes that can live in strong acid. So scientists are thinking about looking in other strange places.

Meteorite ALH 84001 caused a lot of excitement when scientists thought it contained fossilised bacteria. Now they are not so sure.

SCIENCE FACT OR SCIENCE FICTION:
Fossils from Mars?

In 1996, scientists thought they had found evidence of very small bacteria in a Martian **meteorite** named ALH 84001. The meteorite had been found in Antarctica in 1984. Structures within the meteorite looked like primitive living things. Scientists now think that the signs they found were not really evidence of life.

What would life look like on other planets? It's likely that it will look very different to how we imagine it.

Mars

Mars is a good place to start looking for life, because it is the most Earth-like planet. Unlike Venus, there is no dense atmosphere or acid rain. The evidence suggests that there was once liquid water on the planet, and there may still be some underground. Mars is close enough to the Sun for life forms to be able to get their energy from the Sun.

Europa

Jupiter's moon Europa is another place where life may exist. There might be a large watery ocean under the icy surface. Microbes living there could get their energy from the heating caused by the shifting pull of Jupiter's gravity. Alternatively, living things might get energy from chemicals. Some scientists think that Europa is the place where we are most likely to find life.

Changing surfaces

The surfaces of other planets and moons do not stay the same. In the same way that the Earth is always changing, they change too. On planets with an atmosphere, wind and water can change the appearance of the surface. Volcanoes throw out lava, which cools to form new layers of rock. Objects falling onto planets and moons make craters and bring in new materials.

Water

Water is the most destructive form of erosion on Earth. Rivers and oceans alter the shape of the land and rain can dissolve the rocks. Water may also have changed the surface of Mars, as there are features that look like dried-up river beds. Water is an essential ingredient for life on Earth, so scientists are always looking for evidence of water on other planets and moons.

Scientists have found a variety of markings suggesting that there used to be liquid water on the surface of Mars.

TRY IT YOURSELF:
Make a crater

Place a washing-up bowl outside or on a large plastic mat. Half fill the bowl with flour. Use a sieve to lightly cover the surface with cocoa powder. Drop a marble or stone into the bowl, and look at the shape of the crater it makes. Try dropping different-sized objects. Can you find any differences between the craters?

Volcanoes

Volcanoes exist, or have existed, on many bodies in the Solar System. Active volcanoes suggest to scientists that there is heat in the core of the planet. This could be a useful energy source for some forms of life.

The moons Io and Europa are the only places besides Earth where we know there are active volcanoes. Venus and Mars may have active volcanoes, but there is no clear evidence. Venus has over 1100 volcanoes, but it has such a thick atmosphere that it is hard to tell if any of them have erupted recently. On Mars, scientists have recently discovered lava flows that are only a few million years old. There is still a chance that a Martian volcano may erupt again.

Craters

Mercury, Mars, Earth, and Venus are all covered in craters, as are the moons, asteroids, and comets. The craters are caused by meteoroids, asteroids, comets or dust crashing into the surface. When the objects crash, they create craters with rims around them. Outside the rim is all the material that once filled the crater. The objects that made the craters on Earth may have brought some of the chemicals needed for life to our planet.

Jupiter's moon Io is the most volcanic body in the Solar System. The volcanoes on Io send jets of fiery material hundreds of kilometres up into space.

Properties of the planets

Comparison of planetary statistics:

Rocky planets

	Mercury	Venus	Earth	Mars
Rotation period	59 days	243 days	23. 9 hours	24.6 hours
Length of year	88 days	225 days	365.25 days	687 days
Distance from the Sun	58 million km (36 million miles)	108 million km (67 million miles)	150 million km (90 million miles)	228 million km (142 million miles)
Diameter	4880 km (3032 miles)	12,104 km (7521 miles)	12,746 km (7915 miles)	6794 km (4222 miles)
Number of moons	0	0	1	2
Mean surface temperature	167 °C (332 °F)	457 °C (854 °F)	15 °C (59 °F)	−63 °C (−81 °F)
Surface gravity	0.38 (Earth = 1)	0.9 (Earth = 1)	1	0.38 (Earth = 1)

Gas planets

	Jupiter	Saturn	Uranus	Neptune
Rotation period	9.8 hours	10.2 hours	17 hours	16.1 hours
Length of year	12 years	29.5 years	84 years	164 years
Distance from the Sun	779 million km (484 million miles)	1.43 billion km (887 million miles)	2.9 billion km (1.9 billion miles)	4498 million km (2800 million miles)
Diameter	142,984 km (88,848 miles)	120,535 km (74,898 miles)	51,118 km (31,763 miles)	49,528 km (30,775 miles)
Number of moons	at least 63	at least 34	at least 27	at least 13
Mean surface temperature	−108 °C (−162 °F)	−140 °C (−220 °F)	−197 °C (−323 °F)	−200 °C (−328 °F)
Surface gravity	2.36 (Earth = 1)	0.92 (Earth = 1)	0.89 (Earth = 1)	1.1 (Earth = 1)

Pluto

Pluto	
Rotation period	6.4 days
Length of year	248 years
Distance from the Sun	5.9 billion km (3.7 billion miles)
Diameter	2274 km (1413 miles)
Number of moons	1
Mean surface temperature	−215 °C (−356 °F)
Surface gravity	0.06 (Earth = 1)

Glossary

acid chemical that can react with some metals

asteroid minor planet orbiting the Sun

atmosphere gas held by gravity around a planet or moon

atom very tiny particle of matter

axis imaginary axis around which something rotates

bacteria minute living things made up of just one cell

carbon the element that provides the basis for life

carbon dioxide chemical made of carbon and oxygen

comet large block of ice, rock, and dust that orbits the Sun

core the innermost region of a planet

crater hole caused by the impact of a comet or meteorite

crust the solid outer layer of a planet

dense heavy for its size

diameter the width of a circle or sphere

element substance made up of a single kind of atom

elliptical oval in shape

energy property of something that enables it to make a change

equator imaginary line around the middle of a planet, moon, or the Sun

evolve process of gradual change

gravity force that pulls objects together

helium the second lightest gas

hydrogen the lightest gas

magnetic field lines of force around a magnetic object

mantle the layer of a planet or moon between the crust and the core

mass the quantity of matter in an object

meteorite a rock from space that hits the surface of a planet or moon

methane natural gas

microbe tiny life form

molecule two or more atoms joined together

moon rocky body that orbits a planet

nitrogen colourless, odourless gas

organic chemicals carbon-based chemicals

oxygen gas that is important to life

photosynthesis the process by which plants make and store energy

pole one of the two points on a planet or moon, furthest from the equator

radiate to give off energy

rotate turn around on an axis

rotation period the time a planet takes to run round once on its axis

Solar System the planets and their moons, asteroids, comets, meteoroids, etc. that orbit the Sun

Universe the Solar System, stars, the galaxies, and everything between

vaporize to turn a liquid or solid into a gas

water vapour water in the form of a gas

Further information

Books

Cole, Steve. *Space Odyssey: Voyage to the Planets Mission Report* (Dorling Kindersley, 2004)

Couper, Heather, and Henbest, Nigel. *Encyclopedia of Space* (Dorling Kindersley, 2003)

Couper, Heather, and Henbest, Nigel. *Telescopes and Observatories* (Franklin Watts, 1987)

Henbest, Nigel. *The Night Sky* (Usborne, 2000)

Poskitt, Kjartan. *The Gobsmacking Galaxy* (Scholastic, 2004)

Places to visit

Royal Observatory
Greenwich
London
SE10 9NF
UK
+44 (0)20 8312 6565
www.rog.nmm.ac.uk/

Siding Spring Observatory
Coonabarabran
National Park Road
New South Wales
Australia
+64 (0)2 68-426211
www.sidingspringexploratory.com.au

Websites

Hubble gallery *http://hubblesite.org/gallery/*
A gallery of pictures and movies from the Hubble Space Telescope.

SETI@home *http://setiathome.ssl.berkeley.edu/*
Download a screensaver to help look for aliens.

Astronomy Picture of the Day *http://antwrp.gsfc.nasa.gov/apod/astropix.html*
Every day an incredible picture from space and an explanation of what it is and who took the picture. There is an archive of pictures going back to 1995 and an index organized by subject.

Astronomy and the Universe
http://www.windows.ucar.edu/tour/link=/the_universe/the_universe.html
Understanding the sky, constellations, stars, strange objects in space, and much more.

Index

Titles in the *Stargazers' Guides* series include:

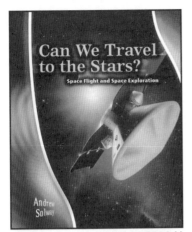

Hardback   0 431 18190 X

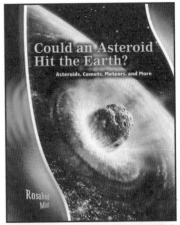

Hardback   0 431 18188 8

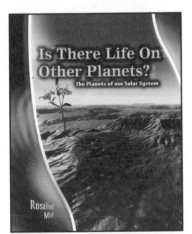

Hardback   0 431 18187 X

Hardback   0 431 18191 8

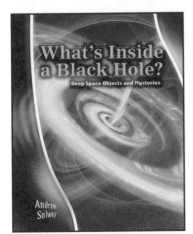

Hardback   0 431 18189 6

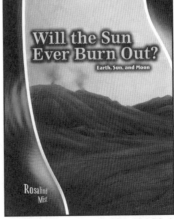

Hardback   0 431 18186 1

Find out about other titles from Heinemann Library on our website www.heinemann.co.uk/library